THE ULTIMATE TRIVIA COLLECTION

THE WORLD'S MOST WEIRD AND WONDERFUL RANDOM FACTS

Graham Cann

Chas Cann Publishers

Copyright © 2023 Graham Cann

ISBN: 978-1-915455-05-5

All rights reserved.

No portion of this book may be reproduced in any form without written permission from the publisher or author, except as permitted by U.S. copyright law.

About the Author

Graham Cann is a #1 bestselling author and joint Director of Chas Cann Publishers **(www.chascannco.com)**.

When he's not scribbling and helping new authors to publish and promote their books, he's singing in a 5-piece band, blood-letting (otherwise known as DIY!) or messing about in kayaks.

You'll often find him walking around the huge network of footpaths that weave in and out of Norfolk villages or meditating on some windswept beach.

https://www.amazon.com/author/grahamcann

Contents

1. Facts That Make You Go "HUH?" — 1
2. Rockin' Through The Ages — 7
3. Do The Scientific Shuffle — 11
4. Historical Eccentricities — 19
5. Rulers And Fools — 25
6. Beetles And Beyond — 31
7. Culinary Capers — 35
8. Believe It Or Not — 45
9. Continents, Customs And Curiosities — 55
10. Artistic Anomalies — 67
11. Sportastic! — 75

12.	Medical Mazes	79
13.	Fast And Furious	87
14.	Creature Feature	91
15.	Eggs-travagant Facts And Fishy Tales	99

YOUR FREE BONUS BOOK

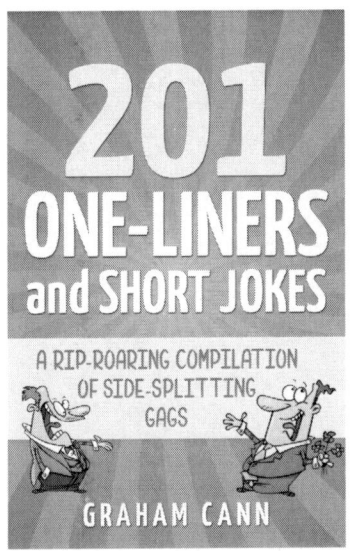

This fantastic **FREE** One-Liner Joke e-Book can be yours!

See more details at the back of this book

"There is much pleasure to be gained from useless knowledge"

Bertrand Russell

Facts That Make You Go "HUH?"

Graveyards and cemeteries are not the same. A graveyard is connected to a church, but a cemetery is not.

The average pencil contains enough graphite to draw a line about 35 miles (56 km) long.

A type of seaweed found in the Pacific Ocean has been known to grow to a length of 600 feet (183 metres).

Ten cows belch enough gas to provide the heating for a small house.

A coprophagist eats dung.

For every human on the planet, there are around 1.6 million ants.

You stand a better chance of dying on your way to buying a lottery ticket than you do of actually winning it.

The name Lego comes from the abbreviation of two Danish words 'leg' and 'godt' which mean 'play well'.

'Rupturewort', a plant used to treat hernias, is the longest word that can be typed using the top row of a keyboard.

Young men fantasise about sex every 15 minutes.

According to a 2016 report, children in the UK spend less time outdoors than prison inmates.

Flirting in public in New York has been illegal since 1902.

The Roman Catholic Church, in an effort to censor statues in Italy, replaced male members with fig leaves. A Vatican curator now guards a secret cellar full of male genitalia.

Man, the higher apes, the guinea pig, the fruit bat and the red-vented bul-bul bird are the only species for whom vitamin C is essential for good health.

The first iPhone was sold in 2007.

You would have to click a mouse around 10 million times to burn one calorie.

Until 1992, electrical appliances in Britain did not have to be sold with plugs, leaving the consumer to attach it themselves.

London's Big Ben is the name of the clock's bell, not the name of the clock tower.

In the third quarter of 2022, 68% of the total wealth in the United States was owned by the top 10% of earners.

Roughly 95% of the oceans remain unexplored by humans.

No word in the English language rhymes with 'month.'

A blob of toothpaste is called a nurdle.

35% of all people using personal ads or online apps for dating are already married. Men are three times more likely to use them than women.

In most advertisements, the time displayed on a watch is 10:10. A study found that this time showed a significantly positive effect on the emotion of the observer and their intent to buy.

The opposite sides of a dice will always add up to seven.

The most common password in 2020 was 123456.

A rhombicuboctahedron is a 26-sided shape.

Super Mario is named after a real-life businessman, Mario Segale, who rented out a warehouse to Nintendo. When Nintendo fell behind paying the rent, Segale did not evict them but gave them a second chance to come up with the money. Nintendo succeeded and named their character after him.

Rockin' Through The Ages

The English horn is neither English nor a horn. It's a French alto oboe.

The study of bells is called campanology.

Despite huge record sales worldwide, not one member of the Beatles could read or write music.

The sound of the 'Doctor Who' Tardis materialising was made by running a set of key along the bass strings of a piano and then playing that sound backwards.

After Ozzy Osbourne left Black Sabbath, Michael Bolton auditioned for the role of the lead singer.

Bagpipes were introduced to Scotland by the Romans.

Mrs Puccini, the wife of the Italian composer, steeped her husband's trousers in camphor and put bromide in his coffee when attractive women came to dinner.

The drummer of Def Leppard only has one arm.

Franz Liszt, the 19th century Hungarian composer, was the first musician reported to have had women's underwear thrown at him.

The Beatles' classic 'Abbey Road' album was originally going to be called 'Everest', as in inside joke after the cigarette brand smoked by engineer, Geoff Emerick. They eventually decided they didn't want to travel all the way to the Himalayas for just one photo shoot.

One of Jennifer Lopez's nicknames in China translates as 'Lord of Butt.'

Frank Zappa, the musician, made a quilt from collecting unwashed panties that were hurled on stage by women during his concerts.

Dolly Parton once took part in a Dolly Parton look-alike contest and lost.

Brian May, Queen's lead guitarist, is an astrophysicist.

The house fly hums in the middle octave key of F.

Violin bows are commonly made from horse hair.

Both drummers from Queen and Duran Duran were called Roger Taylor.

The invention of typing correction fluid is credited to Bette Nesmith Graham. She was the mother of the late Monkees band member, Mike Nesmith.

Bill Clinton excelled as a saxophone player in high school.

DO THE SCIENTIFIC SHUFFLE

Council officials were set a major disposal challenge when a 50 foot whale was washed up on a Lincolnshire beach. The problem was solved when the obliging whale spontaneously exploded.

Hans Asperger identified autism in 1944.

Allergies to Brazil nuts can be passed on sexually.

Researchers in Japan have shown that moderate drinking can improve one's IQ.

Although James Randi offered $1 million US dollars, over a period of more than 50 years, to anyone who could show genuine supernatural or paranormal ability, no-one has ever been able to claim it.

According to NASA, it would take 6 months to travel to Mars.

Breatharianism is the belief that humans can be sustained solely by air and that food and water are not necessary.

In 1967, the world's first UFO landing pad was erected in St. Paul, Alberta, in Canada.

The first electric blanket was invented in 1912 by an American inventor named Samuel Irwin Russell.

The sun contributes 99.87% of the solar system's weight.

The crew of Apollo 15 left a small aluminium plaque on the moon listing astronauts who had died. In 1971, that number was fourteen.

Esther Okade mastered algebra at the age of four and was enrolled in university when she was ten.

Drizzle droplets are roughly one-fiftieth of an inch (.0508 of a cm) in width; fog droplets about one-thousandth of an inch (.00254 of a cm), and raindrops (maximum speed 18mph) about a fifth of an inch (.508 of a cm).

Smells can influence our dreams. A study in 2008 concluded that when volunteers were subjected to scent from roses when they were asleep, nearly all of them had pleasing dreams. The opposite was true when the air was filled with the odour of rotten eggs.

Until 1903, Coca-Cola contained cocaine as an ingredient.

Paradichlorobenzene, once a popular ant killer, is now used in cleaners and deodorisers.

Marie Curie was the first woman to receive a PhD from a French university and the first woman to be employed as a scientist.

A 'jiffy' is actually a measurement of time – 1/100th of a second.

Earth is the only planet in our solar system not named after a Roman god or goddess.

The word 'dinosaur' was first coined by Richard Owen in 1842. It comes from the Greek, 'deinos', meaning fearfully great, and 'sauros', meaning lizard.

The Indian Ocean earthquake and tsunami of 2004 was so powerful it caused the entire planet to vibrate as much as 0.39 inches (1 cm). It was also the longest lasting earthquake ever recorded with a duration of between 8 and 10 minutes.

The giant red spot on Jupiter is actually a storm and is twice as wide as the Earth.

The Great Barrier Reef is the largest living structure in the world and can be seen from the moon.

The gravitational effect of the moon causes the rising and ebbing of the tides on Earth.

Water makes different pouring sounds depending on its temperature.

If you open your eyes in a pitch-black room, the colour you see is 'eigengrau', which is German for intrinsic grey, also known as dark light.

In 10 minutes, a hurricane releases more energy than all the world's nuclear weapons combined.

Hydrogen gas is the least dense substance in the world at 0.08988g/cc.

Venus is the only planet to rotate clockwise.

One of the largest nuclear power accidents occurred at Chernobyl, Ukraine in 1986. Experts have estimated that the area will not be habitable again for at least 3,000 years.

The Eiffel Tower can be 15cm taller in the summer due to thermal expansion.

It would take 19 minutes to fall to the centre of the Earth.

A bolt of lightning can reach 53,540 degrees Fahrenheit. That's 5 times hotter than the surface of the sun.

Humans can only see about 4% of the matter in the universe. The remainder (about 23%) is made up of invisible matter (called Dark Matter) and a mysterious form of energy (about 73%) known as Dark Energy.

All but one of the astronauts who walked on the moon had been Boy Scouts.

Astronauts say that space smells like hot meat.

Historical Eccentricities

In mid 1800s London, smokers discarded 30,000 cigar butts every day.

Albert Einstein never wore socks.

The King owns all the swans in England.

Ella Slack was the body double for Queen Elizabeth II for thirty years.

In the 1920s, a gullible American paid £6,000 for Nelson's Column.

The author Peter Benchley, who wrote *Jaws*, was the US President Lyndon B. Johnson's speechwriter.

Henry VIII's armour has the biggest codpiece in the Tower of London.

Early Wild West first aiders cauterised rattlesnake bites with burning gunpowder.

King Henry II of England once had a jester named Roland the Farter, who would end a dance with a jump, a fart and a whistle in unison.

Ruth Ellis was the last woman to be hanged in Great Britain in 1955.

Margaret Anne Cargill left the largest fortune ever to charity. It totalled $6 billion.

During World War Two, fashion designer Coco Chanel was a spy for the Nazi party.

The armistice, signalling the end of the First World War, was signed on the 11th hour of the 11th day of the 11th month of 1918.

In December 2022 the US national debt stood at $31 trillion.

Elizabeth I kept eighty wigs.

Queen Elizabeth I owned 2000 dresses.

Henry I decreed that the yard should be the distance from his nose to his outstretched thumb.

Bermondsey in London had one lavatory for every 25 houses in 1898.

Until the 16th century, bodies of the wealthy were buried inside churches in England and paupers buried outside. The inscription on a gravestone at Kingsbridge, Devon reads; 'Here I lie at the chancel door, Here I lie because I'm poor. The further in, the more you'll pay, Here I lie as warm as they.'

The Ancient Egyptians were devoted to their pets. When a beloved cat died, they shaved off their eyebrows as a sign of mourning. When a dog died, they shaved their whole body.

Violet Jessop was the lucky ship's nurse, who worked on the Brittanic, the Olympic and the Titanic. The Olympic collided with a warship and nearly sank: the Brittanic hit a mine and sank; the Titanic hit an iceberg and went under.

In 1710, there were more than 500 coffee houses in London, taking up more premises than any other trade in the city.

It was the height of fashion in the 17th century to tint the lips green or black.

Robert Spears, who pleaded self-defence, was acquitted of murdering a man and throwing his body into the Ohio River. After the verdict, he was charged again, this time for littering the river.

The first king of England, Alfred the Great, made a law that everyone had to be in bed by 8pm.

Until 2007, slavery was legal in Mauritania. Even still, 1-4% of the population are still living as slaves.

Britain's first public flushing toilet for women opened in the Strand in London on 11th February 1852. Only 82 women used it in the first 12 months.

In 16th century England, chimneys were a status symbol.

Rulers And Fools

MI5 once planned to use gerbils to detect terrorists. The only problem was that the gerbils couldn't differentiate between terrorists and passengers who were afraid of flying.

The US Navy uses dolphins and sea lions to detect underwater mines.

Place settings at Buckingham Palace banquets are measured with a ruler.

The US Government's *Infant Care* publication in 1914 recommended that peat moss be used for disposable nappies.

Renegade was President Obama's Secret Service code name.

It's illegal to ride an ugly horse in Wilbur, Washington US.

The British Army abandoned the lance as an operational weapon in 1927.

To overcome the boredom at a particularly gruelling reception, President Truman uttered to everyone he met: 'I murdered my grandmother this morning.' No-one took any notice except one man who replied: 'She had it coming to her.'

James Madison was the 4th President of the United States and the shortest at only 5 feet 4 inches (1.63 metres) tall.

Mr Lancashire was president of the Blackpool branch of the Yorkshire Association.

Until 1879, soldiers in the British Army, who were found guilty of wrongdoing, were tattooed with the initials B.C. (Bad Character).

One of Richard Nixon's re-election slogans in 1972 was: 'They Can't Lick Our Dick'.

The Groom of the Stool was the most intimate of an English monarch's attendants, responsible for assisting the King in excretion and hygiene.

Hot and cold running water was pioneered by the first Duke of Devonshire.

As a child, Adolf Hitler wanted to be a priest.

President Abraham Lincoln suffered from severe depression.

The Houses of Parliament covers eight acres, has more than 1000 rooms, over 100 staircases and two miles of passages.

Stalin's first son shot himself because of his father's harshness towards him, but he survived. Stalin stated, 'He can't even shoot straight.

Prince Charles became the first member of the Royal Family to become a blood donor on 1st March 1985.

Winston Churchill had the same governess, Miss Hutchinson, as another future British Prime Minister, Clement Attlee.

Donald Trump has his own set of emojis called "Trumpmojis" that feature his various facial expressions and gestures.

In 1845, US President Jackson's parrot was removed from his funeral for swearing.

Beetles And Beyond

If a common house spider was scaled up in size and speed, it could give a world beating sprinter an eight second start over 100 metres, and still reach the finish line before him.

The wood frog can hold its pee for up to 8 months.

Snails can sleep for 3 years.

Leopard frogs use their eyes to help them swallow.

Around 2 billion people around the world eat insects as part of their daily meals.

A praying mantis can camouflage itself by changing colour from dark brown to green depending on its background.

The inch-long Colombian tree frog contains enough venom for fifty poisoned arrows.

An unusual storm showered more than 100,000 small toads on the village of Brignoles in France.

There is a cryptid that's believed to exist in the Gobi Desert called the Mongolian Death Worm. It can grow in length to 60 inches (1.5 metres) and kills its prey with electric shocks from its eyes.

Giant anteaters tongues can extend out of their mouths up to 2 feet (610 mm).

Most species of gecko will shed their tails if tugged, as a defence mechanism.

Half a million locusts – a small fraction of an average swarm – consume as much food in a day as 250 people.

Tarantulas can live for two and a half years without food.

After mating, a male bee's testicles explode and it dies.

A snail can have up to 25,600 teeth.

A parasitic worm lives under a hippopotamus's eyelids and lives on tears.

It takes 2 million flower visits for bees to produce a single pound of honey.

An athletic snail, travelling at its optimum speed of 2 inches per minute, could complete the Olympic marathon in 550 days.

The American cicada mates only once in his 17 year life, and dies immediately afterwards.

If they all survived and multiplied, at the end of one year, the descendants of one aphid would weigh as much as 600 million men.

A snail is equipped with both male and female reproductive organs on its head.

A mature oak tree can have as many as 400,000 caterpillars living in it.

Culinary Capers

When peeling potatoes, men use 2.7 calories of energy per minute and women use 1.29.

A Frenchman murdered two of his wives because he was dissatisfied with their cooking.

A sample of chicken tested at a Subway in Canada was found to have 50% chicken and the remainder was soy filler.

2.5 tins of spam are eaten every second in the US.

Coffee is the most traded commodity after petroleum.

Arachibutyrophobia is the fear of getting peanut butter stuck to the roof of your mouth.

McDonald's once made bubble-gum flavoured broccoli.

The popular sweet brand, M&M's, stands for *Mars* and *Murrie*.

Turophobia is the fear of cheese.

In Ancient Greece, senior citizens living on the island of Kea were expected to drink poisonous hemlock on their 60th birthday.

The greengage was introduced into England by Sir William Gage in 1725.

Argentine gauchos sometimes place slices of raw beef underneath their saddles. After a hard day's ride, the meat is tenderised and cooked by the heat.

Monkey brains are considered a delicacy in parts of South Asia, Africa and China.

About 50% of Asians have problems metabolising alcohol because they are missing a liver enzyme that's needed to process it.

Watermelon is composed of up to 92% water. It is a good choice if you want to keep hydrated or lose weight because it is low in calories.

Kalsarikannit is a word in Finnish which means to get drunk in your underwear at home.

When muffs reached their most fashionable extremes in the 16th century, spoon handles had to be lengthened.

After banquets at Buckingham Palace, the dirty plates had to be returned to the kitchen using leather buckets to save the gold from scratching.

Colonel Sanders, who created KFC, began the franchise when he was 65.

In Thailand, rats are considered a delicacy.

Madagascar and Indonesia produce two-thirds of the world's supply of vanilla.

Because Hindus don't eat beef, McDonald's in New Delhi makes its burgers from mutton.

In the early development of New York, one house in four sold alcohol.

When a bar in California offered 'all the beer you can drink for a dollar', Glenn Moore drank 16 pints in four hours and died.

The Snickers chocolate bar was named after the favourite horse of the Mars family.

In 2016, France became the first country to ban supermarkets from throwing away unsold food, forcing them to donate it instead.

Clarence Birdseye first got the idea of selling frozen food when he dined with natives of Labrador on caribou, which had been frozen in the Arctic ice.

A micro-brewery is independently owned and creates no more than 15,000 barrels of beer a year.

The new dining experience is 'Dinner in the Sky' where you are hoisted over 100 feet (30 metres) on a platform table and this is where you enjoy your meal. Should you need to visit the toilet, the device is lowered but you cannot continue the session.

In a survey, 7% of American adults believe that chocolate milk comes from brown cows.

Between 1940 and 1945, the rabbit made up 10% of Britain's meat ration.

In 1994, Tom Berenger, along with Lisa and Debbie Ganz, launched a restaurant called 'Twins', which was staffed by 29 sets of identical twins.

You can buy eel flavoured ice cream in Japan.

If you yelled for 8 years, 7 months and 6 days, you would have produced enough sound energy to heat one cup of coffee.

Americans, on average, eat 18 acres (7.28 hectares) of pizza every day.

When Fredric J. Baur, who invented Pringles, was cremated, a portion of his ashes were buried in an original flavour Pringles container.

Astronauts are not allowed to eat beans before blast off because passing wind damages spacesuits.

A chef's hat has 100 pleats and were said to represent the number of ways the chef wearing it could cook an egg.

Japan has over 300 flavours of Kit Kats, including banana, baked potato and blueberry cheesecake.

A single strand of spaghetti is called a spaghetto.

Costa coffee employs Gennaro Pelliccia as a coffee taster, who has had his tongue insured for £10 million since 2009.

Lettuce is a member of the sunflower family.

In China and Japan, it's considered polite to slurp your soup.

The world record for eating cockroaches is 36 in a minute and was achieved by retired rat catcher Ken Edwards in 2001.

Pieter Bruegel the Elder's 1559 painting The Fight Between Carnival and Lent, includes one of the first known images of waffles.

Chocolate contains a chemical theobromine, which is poisonous to dogs. It affects their heart and nervous system.

In 1990, the European Union ruled that carrots can be classified as fruit because they can be made into jam.

Believe It Or Not

In Sweden, you can buy toilet paper called 'Krapp'.

It's illegal to wrestle a bear in South Africa.

Anatidaephobia is the term used when people fear they are being watched by ducks.

Play-Doh began as a wallpaper cleaner in the 1930s.

To keep pongs to a minimum, you can actually buy flatulence deodoriser pads.

According to Guinness World Records, Anthony Victor has the longest ear hair ever recorded measuring 7 inches (18 cms).

Thousands of yellow plastic ducks fell from a cargo ship in the Pacific Ocean in 1992. Many have been sighted in various locations around the world for the last 30 years.

It's illegal to pass wind in Malawi.

The number four is the only number with the same amount of letters.

Stewardesses is the longest word that can be typed using just the left hand on a keyboard.

In 2016, Apple reached one billion iPhone sales.

Two thirds of humans are not aware of what they are good at and what their strengths are, according to the Journal of Positive Psychology.

Clowns copyright their styles of make-up by painting the design on eggshells, which are stored in the vaults of the International Circus Club in Paris.

A Los Angeles school board tried to ban Tarzan books because the hero lived with Jane in a tree house and they weren't married.

Only 5% of Norway's financial transactions are completed using cash.

Allan Ganz holds the world record for the longest serving ice cream man. He started in 1947 in the greater Boston area and knows 90% of his customers by name.

Triskaidekaphobia is the fear of the number 13.

The video game Minecraft was sold to Microsoft in 2015 for $2.5 billion.

Vincent Castiglia is an American artist who paints exclusively with human blood.

Graffito' is the singular word for graffiti.

14.5 billion electronic messages received every day are spam.

A letter posted in Bromley in Kent arrived 37 years later at Thorogood, Sutton-at-Hone 12 miles away. The Post Office demanded 6p excess postage.

People fall asleep in 7 minutes, on average.

1 in 5 adults believes that aliens hide on the planet in human form, according to a 2010 Reuters global survey.

A dairy in Suffolk, in the United Kingdom, collected 1800 empty milk bottles from the home of a single elderly lady.

Cherophobia is an aversion to happiness.

Rob Ross, the TV artist from the *Joy of Painting*, never earned a cent from the TV programme itself, but made money selling from his art supply store.

Koumpounophobia is the fear of buttons.

The average family loses up to 60 socks a year.

Two women in Louisville, Kentucky, inherited an estate worth $115,000 from their late aunt's goat.

According to a study, the average woman owns 34 pairs of knickers.

Pteronophobia is the fear of being tickled by feathers.

The raincoat was invented by Charles Macintosh in 1824 in Scotland.

A pangram is a sentence that contains all the letters of the alphabet such as 'the quick brown fox jumps over the lazy dog.'

In 1993, Karl Watkins of Worcestershire, England, was jailed for having sex with pavements.

Agalmatophilia describes sexual arousal evoked by a statue, doll or mannequin.

The '&' symbol is known as an ampersand.

A merkin is a woman's pubic wig.

A survey carried out by a wig-maker revealed that 51% of male wearers thought their false thatch gave them more sex appeal and more than a third believed it improved their performance in bed.

The letters SIM in sim cards stands for Subscriber Identity Module.

During our lives, we spend, on average, 5 years and 3 months on social media.

It's illegal to sell chewing gum in Singapore.

The dot above the letter 'i' is called a tittle.

Edwin Tobergta of Hamilton, Ohio, was arrested in October 2002 for having sex with an inflatable pumpkin.

Georgia O'Keeffe's paintings of flowers have been regarded as depictions of female genitalia.

The King of Hearts is the only king in a deck of cards without a moustache.

Fully stretched out, Slinkies can be up to 82 feet (25 metres) long.

Another name for the symbol # is an octothorpe.

The Guiness World Record for the longest time spent searching for the Loch Ness Monster is held by Steve Feltham, who camped at Loch Ness for 25 years.

Webster's Dictionary had the word 'dord' in it for 5 years before it was noticed that it was not actually a word at all and had been accidentally added.

The average person glances at their smartphone 150 times a day.

The world's first Valentine message is believed to have been sent by Margery Brews of Norfolk to her fiance, John Paston, in 1477.

The average life span of an umbrella is 1.5 years.

The name given to the line that separates the top and bottom numbers of a fraction, is called a vinculum.

The first email was sent in 1971 by Ray Tomlinson to himself.

The plastic tube at the end of a shoelace is called an aglet.

Continents, Customs And Curiosities

Scientists In Russia found a live reptile in a chunk of Siberian ice 33 feet below ground level.

Builders in Japan once used kites to transport bricks to the top of tall buildings.

Every pint of water from the Dead Sea contains 4oz of salt.

If the population of China walked past you in single file, the line would never end due to the rate of reproduction.

Marco Polo introduced rhubarb to Europe from the court of the Chinese Emperor Kublai Khan.

In Japan, it's illegal to commit suicide by jumping in front of a train.

In Tuszyn, Poland, officials opposed naming a park after Winnie the Pooh because he goes round half naked.

There's a community in Holland called Dementia Village where every inhabitant has dementia. It has normal amenities like shops and restaurants but has a secure perimeter so everyone is free to roam.

Due to an ancient custom, when a Peruvian woman finds an unusually ugly potato, she goes up to the nearest man and smashes it in his face.

There is a website called African where you can watch live footage of wildlife living in protected areas in southern Africa.

'Husband Storage' is a term used in a Chinese mall, where wives can leave their husbands while they do their shopping.

In China, ground bees are used as a remedy for a sore throat.

A blonde Venezuelan stripper who performed nightly at a club in Caracas, wrote to her mother every week enclosing a doctor's certificate to show she was still a virgin.

In pre-war Japan, the Emperor was too sacrosanct to be touched. Even his tailor had to estimate his imperial dimensions at a distance of several yards.

Abu Dhabi runs a beauty contest for camels.

Angel Falls in Venezuela is the highest waterfall in the world at 3,212 feet (979 metres).

An 82-year-old Ukranian woman discovered her long-lost wedding ring inside the 1973 Christmas turkey. The diamond and gold ring slipped from her finger while working on the family farm in 1914.

An Indian maharajah had a bed guarded at each corner by a realistic life-size nude robot. His weight triggered off a musical box which made the mechanical ladies fan his face and feet in time to the music.

American Indian fathers name their children by taking a look at their newly born child and then stepping outside and naming the first thing they see. For example, Flying Cloud, Laughing Water, Sitting Bull.

A girl's boarding school at Fettan, Switzerland, had to be closed for a fortnight in the 1920s while the girls recovered from a general mania brought on by the attractiveness of one of the female teachers.

An Australian student was arrested on a charge of offensive behaviour for walking down the street dressed as a sealion.

The only continent not to have rabies is the Antarctic, according to the World Health Organisation.

In La Crosse, Kansas, there is a museum of barbed wire.

Duffel bags are named after the town Duffel in Belgium, where the bags were first made.

Siberia covers 77 per cent of Russia. If it were independent, it would be the largest country in the world.

Antarctica has 24 hours of sunlight during the summer and 24 hours of darkness in the winter.

The smallest country in the world is Vatican City. It takes up 0.17 square miles (0.44 square kilometres) and is an independent state surrounded by Rome.

In 2007, Scotland spent £125,000 devising a new national slogan. The winning entry was 'Welcome to Scotland'.

Following its success at raising attendances in Sunday School, a 5-foot robot, with a voice like a Dalek and red eyes which flashed as it spoke, was wheeled in to read the lessons during adult services at the Elim Pentecostal Church in Nottingham.

The Chinese used fingerprints for identification in 700AD.

Nyepi is a day of silence celebrated every Balinese New Year. Security men walk the streets silencing everyone to fool evil spirits that all the people have left.

After the death and discredit of Beria, chief of the secret police, Russians were told to tear out any references to him in their encyclopaedias and replace them with an entry about the Bering Sea.

The Machineel tree of the Caribbean and Gulf of Mexico is the world's most dangerous tree. Its sap can cause blisters or blindness. You can't eat it, touch it, or burn it without injury.

The annual Monkey Buffet Festival in Thailand provides food and drink to the local monkey inhabitants, thanking them for attracting tourists to the town.

The Australian state of Tasmania has the cleanest air in the world.

Dublin, Ireland is home to The National Leprechaun Museum.

In 2005, security guards at Australia's Parliament House were banned from calling people 'mate'. The ban lasted one day.

In Finland, they have 'National Sleepy Head Day', where the last person in a family to wake up is thrown by the rest of them into a lake or the sea.

The largest recorded earthquake was in Chile in 1960. It measured 9.5 magnitude.

A male prisoner at America's San Quentin jail filed a law suit in a US district court, demanding the removal of two women guards because their presence constituted 'cruel and unusual punishment.'

Canada is more than twice the size of the entire European Union.

Petaluma in California has been holding the world's ugliest dog contest since the 1970s.

Australia has a larger population of camels than Egypt.

In the US state of Oregon, there stands a phallic stone formation which was called 'Cock Rock'. It has since been renamed to placate sensitive souls.

In China, 'virgin boy eggs' are considered a delicacy. The eggs are boiled in the urine of young virgin boys under 10 years old.

The Emperor Maximilian ordered the two rivals for his daughter's hand to fight a duel, the winner being the one to place the other inside a large bag.

The unicorn is the national animal of Scotland.

The Main Library at Indiana University in the US sinks over an inch every year because engineers failed to account for the weight of all the books that it would eventually hold.

The world's longest walking distance is 14,000 miles. From Magadan in Russia to Cape Town in South Africa requires no flying or sailing.

In China, rich people hire body doubles to serve their prison sentences.

Iceland does not have a railway station.

IKEA is an acronym that stands for Ingvar Kamprad Elmtaryd Agunnaryd, which is the founder's name, the farm where he grew up, and his hometown.

St Lucia is the only country in the world named after a woman.

The word kimono literally means a thing to wear. Ki is 'wear' and mono is 'thing'.

Norway has a 25-year statute of limitaition on murder. This means if the murder happened more than 25 years ago, they cannot be charged.

Between North and South Korea lies 155 miles (249.44m) of no man's land, where hundreds of rare animal species thrive.

The Great Pyramid of Giza actually has 8 sides rather than 4.

The biggest religious building in the world is a Hindu temple, Angkor Wat, located in Cambodia. It actually features on the Cambondia flag, the only building to appear on any national flag.

The cash machines in Vatican City are the only ones in the world to have Latin as a language display option.

Of the 8 billion people now living on planet Earth, most live in China (1.439 billion), followed by India (1.80 billion).

So much water floods from the Amazon into the Atlantic that ships out of sight of land can draw up fresh water.

Artistic Anomalies

Alfred Hitchcock's film *Psycho* was made in black and white to make the famous shower scene more bearable and to help get it past the censors.

Jayne Mansfield and Marie Antoinette had exactly the same bust sizes.

Stephen King chucked the first pages of his manuscript *Carrie* into the bin in sheer frustration but his wife urged him to keep going.

The woman who starred in the film *I Am Frigid* was billed as 'Sandra Julien', of *I am a Nymphomaniac* fame.

As a young teenager, while filming *The Wizard of Oz*, Judy Garland was said to have been miserable on set after being repeatedly molested by Munchkins who put their hands up her dress.

Carrie Fisher never wore a bra in her Princess Leia costume.

The film *The Hunger Games* is banned in Vietnam because of its violence.

The famous children's author Roald Dahl wrote the screenplay for the James Bond film *You Only Live Twice*.

Psycho (1960) was the first American film to feature a flushing toilet, which was quite shocking at the time for US audiences.

'Elementary, my dear Watson' was never actually coined by Sherlock Holmes in the books written by Sir Arthur Conan Doyle.

The Wolf of Wall Street has the greatest number of swear words of any film ever produced.

The role of Captain Jack Sparrow was originally offered to Jim Carrey but he turned it down for the role of Bruce Almighty.

It is reported that Robert Louis Stevenson wrote *Dr Jekyll and Mr Hyde* while on a six-day cocaine binge.

The Oxford English Dictionary credits Charles Dickens with the first use of the words *butter-fingers, crossfire, dustbin, fairy story, slow-coach* and *whoosh* among many others.

Kuwait banned the 2017 film *Beauty and the Beast* because of the character, LeFou, who was gay.

Wagner wore pink underwear.

Clarkstown, New Jersey, appointed a 60-year-old blind man to be its chief cinema censor.

Toto, the dog in the *Wizard of Oz* (1939), was paid $125 per week, more than the Munchkin actors.

Author Charles Dickens held the belief that facing north while sleeping helped to increase his creativity. He carried a compass with him to ensure that he was facing in the right direction.

Edward Nigma or E. Nigma was the Riddler's real name in the Batman stories.

The first crossword puzzle in Britain was published by the Sunday Express in 1924.

On one slow news day on 18th April 1930, a BBC radio announcer blatantly said, 'There is no news'.

The first novel written on a typewriter is said to have been Mark Twain's 'Adventures Of Tom Sawyer' in 1876.

The average young person in the US is exposed to 13000 to 30000 advertisements just on television each year.

Dopey is the only vertically challenged man in Disney's 'Snow White and the Seven Dwarfs' not to wear a beard.

As an author in Norway, depending on your book meeting certain criteria, the government will buy 1000 copies for use in libraries.

In the 1999 movie, The Matrix, Neo's passport expires on 11 September 2001.

In 1905, when 70-years-old, Mark Twain began to collect a bevy of adolescent girls, whom he called his "angel-fish." He defended his predilection by insisting that he longed for grandchildren.

A bookshop in the fashionable London suburb of Hampstead, in an effort to reduce shoplifting, pinned up the notice: 'Children of progressive parents not admitted.'

Dr Seuss invented the word 'nerd'. It appeared in a book called If I Ran the Zoo in 1950. The word's meaning in the book referred to a comically unpleasant creature but now means someone with an obsessive interest in something.

The girl's name Wendy was first coined by J.M. Barrie in Peter Pan in 1904.

Elvis Presley was originally blonde. He started colouring his hair for an edgier look and sometimes used to touch it up with boot polish.

Berry Berenson, the wife of Anthony Perkins, the original Norman Bates, died as a result of being a passenger on one of the 9/11 planes.

After the release of the 1996 film Scream, which involved an anonymous killer calling and murdering his victims, Caller ID usage tripled in America.

Ten years after John Logie Baird gave the first demonstration of television in 1926 in London, there were only 100 TV sets in the world.

Samuel J. Seymour, the last surviving witness of the assassination of Abraham Lincoln, lived long enough to be interviewed on national television in 1956.

Nosmo King, the British music hall artist, hit upon his stage name as he walked through a pair of swing doors bearing the instruction 'No Smoking'.

The Wilhelm Scream is a stock sound effect of a man screaming that has been used in a number of films and TV series, beginning in 1951 with the film 'Distant Drums'.

Sportastic!

Two football teams comprised of completely blind players drew 2-2 in Lima, Peru using a sonic ball which had been filled with a handful of dried peas.

The top marbles team, the Toucan Terribles, ground their own marbles out of lavatory bowls.

During an amateur football match in Mexico City, after an argument with a goalkeeper, who disputed a goal, the centre forward went off to the dressing room, returned with a pistol and riddled him with bullets.

Exercising increases productivity. A regular exercise regime can make you happier, smarter and more energetic.

The winner of the annual worm championship races in California is the first competitor to cover a circle with a 3 foot (91 cms) radius.

Angelo Faticoni, the Human Cork, swam from Manhattan to Hoboken tied in a chair weighted with 40 lb. (18 kg) of lead.

In 1921, the Football Association banned ladies' soccer and they were not officially allowed back on to the pitch until fifty years later in 1971.

The North Pole hosts the coldest marathon on Earth every year. Runners have to dress in thermal layers, windproof trousers, and goggles.

John Faulkner, the world's oldest jockey, rode his final race at the age of 74, a steeplechase in Abingdon, England.

Before the introduction of the whistle in the early 1870s, soccer referees waved a white handkerchief.

Shirley Crabtree was better known as the professional English wrestler, Big Daddy.

The Olympic Acceptance Board received an application from the Gumboot Olympic Committee for recognition of their sport. Their spokesman was Australian, Ron Payton, holder of the Silver Welly, who had pitched a gumboot 111.3 feet, beating the previous world record by one inch.

Antanas Kontrimas of Lithuania set the record for the heaviest weight lifted by a human beard. In 2013, Antanas lifted 63.80 kg using just his beard.

The current holder for the world's longest fart is a man called Bernard Clemmens or Mr Methane of London. He managed to let off one continuous fart for exactly 2 minutes and 42 seconds.

The average number of dimples on a golf ball is 336. The dimples vibrate the air around the ball when it's in the air, reducing the drag, making the ball go further.

Cheetahs were raced at London's Romford Greyhound Stadium in 1937.

The loudest known grunt at Wimbledon came from Maria Sharapova during the 2009 tennis tournament, recorded at about 105 decibels, the equivalent of standing 3 feet (0.91 metres) from a motorcycle.

Medical Mazes

It's not possible to breathe and swallow simultaneously.

It's impossible for most people to lick their own elbow.

When you get red eyes after swimming in a pool, health research has shown that it's not due to the chlorine, but the result of urine, faeces and sweat in the water.

In the late 1800s, tampons laced with cocaine were all the rage, claiming to be the cure for everything.

In Ancient Egypt, they used to inject red lead, goat urine, ant eggs and bat wings into the ear canal to help cure hearing loss.

Every sixth death in the world is caused by cancer.

Two hundred thousand frowns make one wrinkle.

100 people choke to death on ballpoint pen caps every year.

'Continuum' was a magazine that denied the existence of HIV/AIDS. It stopped being published in 2001 after all its editorial staff had died of AIDS.

The oldest authenticated age of any human is 122.

Everyone's tongue print is unique.

During the 1950s, pregnant women were advised that smoking while pregnant was entirely safe.

People used to believe that kissing a donkey could relieve toothache.

A Swedish doctor weighed patients before and after death and calculated that a human soul weighed 0.046 lbs (21g).

Marijuana was prescribed by Chinese physicians as a remedy for gout, rheumatism, malaria, beri-beri and absent-mindedness.

Every time you take a step forward, you use 54 muscles.

You breathe about 8,409,600 times in a year.

Dysania is the word used to describe people who have difficulty waking up and getting out of bed in the mornings.

A photic sneeze reflex is where people sneeze when they look at the sun. It's also called Autosomal Dominant Compelling Helio-Opthalmic Outburst syndrome or ADCHOO for short.

In 1988, an extreme bout of hiccups was remedied by rectal massage.

Victoria Beckham used to dress up as a sperm for a BBC sex education show before becoming Posh Spice.

A British dentist left nearly £200,000 to his nurse, stipulating that she did not wear any make-up or go out with men for five years after his death.

Viruses can get viruses.

The medical condition, synesthesia, can cause sufferers to taste the words they hear.

Some people believe they can read your fortune by examining your faeces.

Tonic water was once a common medicine for combatting malaria.

Only 2% of the world's population has green eyes.

The buttock muscle, gluteus maximus, is the largest in the human body.

Pneumonoultramicroscopicsilicovolcanoconiosis is the longest word in the English language. It is a lung disease.

Fregoli Delusion is the belief that everybody you meet is the same person in disguise.

Hikikomori is a form of severe social withdrawal affecting millions of Japanese men characterised by adolescents and young adults who become recluses in their parents' homes, unable to work or go to school for months or years.

Your ears never stop growing during your entire lifetime.

The loudest male burp ever recorded, according to the Guinness Book of Records, was 112.4 decibels. It was achieved by Australian, Neville Sharp on 29th July 2021.

A dentist named Alfred P. Southwick, first invented the electric chair in 1881.

The human heart creates enough pressure when it pumps out of the body to squirt blood 30 feet (9 metres).

Your fingernails grow faster on your dominant hand.

Human teeth are the only part of the human body that cannot heal itself.

Women blink nearly twice as much as men.

After a beheading, you can still be conscious for up to 10 seconds afterwards.

When lovers gaze into each other's eyes, their heartbeats pound in unison.

All human embryos begin as females in the womb. That's why men have nipples.

Pandiculating occurs when you yawn and stretch at the same time.

The phrase 'elimination communication' is where, instead of using nappies, the parent learns to use timing, signals and cues to know when their baby is about to pee or poo.

The first successful penis transplant was carried out in 2016. The surgery lasted 15 hours.

Your body contains about 100,00 miles of blood vessels.

Fast And Furious

The first commercial use of Bakelite was in the making of gear knobs for Rolls-Royces.

It's illegal in London to flag down a taxi if you have the plague.

In 1912, London's 2500 buses were driven so recklessly that they killed one pedestrian every two days.

The parking meter was invented by C. C. Magee in 1935.

A London clergyman, who was run down by a lorry, was awarded £8000 in damages because he claimed he could no longer kneel to pray.

At Beachy Head in the UK, during one particularly dramatic instance in August 2008, a car plunged over the cliff, speeding past a rescue team, while they were still busy retrieving the body of a previous jumper.

On applying for car insurance, an elderly man once admitted to three accidents. His car had been hit by an aircraft; had been rammed by a yacht and swamped by a giant wave.

It is illegal to slam your car door in Switzerland.

In Nashville, Tennessee, there is a vending machine that dispenses real cars. It has five storeys and is fully automated.

The first aeroplane flew on 17th December 1903 by Wilbur and Orville Wright.

The average person spends 6 months of their lifetime waiting at red traffic lights.

When London held a Treasures of Tutankhamun exhibition in 1972, a taxi driver was alleged to have taken a man to Tooting Common by mistake.

Introduced in 1966, the Toyota Corolla was the first mass-market car to have a radio fitted as standard.

In Japan, some trains have windows that can be opened partially to accommodate the "pusher" staff whose job is to literally push passengers into crowded trains during rush hours.

The world's fastest recorded speed on a public road is 277.87 mph (447.19 km/h) achieved by a Bugatti Veyron Super Sport in 2010.

The average person spends about 38 hours each year stuck in traffic.

CREATURE FEATURE

Rabbits are born naked but hares are born with fur.

The warning sign of an orangutan is a raucous belch.

A giraffe's tongue can be 20 inches (51cms) long.

Dalmatian puppies are born with pure white coats.

The hippopotamus has the largest canines of any land animal measuring 16 inches (40cm) long.

A little known Sardinian sheep's milk cheese, casu marzu, contains live maggots.

The reason why poison works so well with rats is that they are unable to vomit.

Gestation for African elephants lasts an average of 22 months.

Nose prints of dogs are unique, rather like fingerprints in humans.

The spines of baby hedgehogs are soft and flexible.

A hamster can only blink one eye at a time.

Male capuchin monkeys urinate on their hands and bodies in order to attract females.

Wombat poo is cube-shaped.

It's impossible for a pig to look up into the sky.

The sloth, the world's slowest mammal, manages to camouflage itself in trees thanks to a green algae that grows on its coat.

A group of hippos is called a crash.

Dogs feel more vulnerable while they are excreting. That's why they look at their owners for protection.

If you want to escape from a charging bull, run downhill. Its front legs are shorter than its back legs which means it can run faster uphill.

A group of pandas is called an embarrassment.

A study once found that, while sober, rats prefer silence, but on cocaine, they prefer jazz.

A group of ferrets is called a business.

Sloths spend an average of 10 hours every week awake but motionless; 11 hours feeding; 18 hours climbing; and 129 hours asleep.

In December 1963, a Florida police patrol picked up a chimpanzee for speeding. It turned out to be a hoax. A hidden carnival showman was working the pedals with the chimp steering.

A monkey washed ashore at Hartlepool, Co. Durham during the Napoleonic Wars was mistaken by townspeople for a French spy. The poor animal was tried and hanged.

A pig's orgasm can last up to 30 minutes.

Goats have rectangular pupils.

Kangaroos are 1 inch (2.54 cms) at birth and grow to 8 feet (2.44 metres).

Jackrabbits are hares and not rabbits. Hares can run at around 40mph (64km/h) and jump as high as 10 feet (3 metres).

Beavers are able to hold their breath underwater for up to 15 minutes.

The only domestic animal not mentioned in the Bible is a cat.

Giraffes are especially prone to throat infections because they are not able to cough.

An elephant's skin can be up to 1 inch (2.54 cm) thick but so sensitive that it can detect a fly landing on it.

Domestic cats purr at around 26 cycles per second, which is roughly the same frequency as an idling diesel engine.

A group of buffalo is called an obstinacy.

As a defence mechanism, horned lizards expel blood from their eyes.

Koala bears are marsupials, not bears.

The Australian white-throated snapping turtle, can breathe through its anus.

Congo, the chimpanzee, is considered the greatest animal painter in history. In 2005, three of his works were included in an auction together with Warhol and Renoir, and they sold for $26,000.

Flamingoes are naturally white, but change colour to pink due to their diet of shrimps, algae and crustaceans.

Bulls are partially colour-blind compared to humans. It's a fallacy that they are lured by the colour red. It's motion that attracts them.

Giraffes can go longer without water than camels can.

Tigers have striped skin as well as striped fur.

There are 32 muscles in a cat's ear.

Border collies are considered to be the most intelligent breed of dog.

A crocodile cannot stick out its tongue.

Most pandas in the world are on loan from China.

Basenji dogs are the only breed that don't bark. The noise they make is more like a yodel.

Baby rabbits are called kits.

Eggs-travagant Facts And Fishy Tales

An endling is the name given to the last one of a single species before extinction occurs.

Flamingos can fly at a speed of 35 miles an hour (56 kilometres an hour).

Owls are unable to move their eyes left and right and, instead, have to turn their heads to look sideways. Some owls can manage to turn their heads 270 degrees.

A chicken egg has more than 7000 pores which allow a chick to inhale oxygen and exhale carbon dioxide.

Penguins can create enough speed underwater to leap 7 feet (2 metres) or more into the air.

An albatross can glide for up to six days without beating its wings.

Bats always exit a cave to the left.

During the Middle Ages, pigeons were the main source of fresh meat in Britain.

A puffin eats the equivalent of its own body weight in 24 hours.

A pair of sparrows make around 5000 hunting trips during the three week period before their chicks fly the nest.

Thousands of sparrows were killed because they were seen as pests during Mao's China in 1958. As the sparrows became less, so the locust and other insect populations increased, ravaging crops and causing the Great Chinese Famine, which killed up to 45 million people.

A penguin, known only as 337, escaped from the Tokyo Sea Life Park and found freedom in Tokyo Bay. He managed to climb a 13 foot wall and scramble through a barbed wire fence. He was recaptured after 82 days.

Swans have one partner for life. In some cases, when one swan dies, its partner dies from a broken heart.

The official name of Twitter's logo was Larry the bird, named after the Hall of Fame NBA player, Larry Bird.

Squids suffering from depression in captivity commit suicide by eating their own tentacles.

The blood of an eel is poisonous and can kill a human.

Some lobsters can live up to 50 years or more.

Adult dolphins have a mental age equivalent to that of a seven-year-old child.

A humpback whale can eat 5000 fish at a single sitting.

The octopus has three hearts.

The giant squid has the biggest eye of any living creature, bigger than a man's head.

After the world fishing exhibition in Vigo, Spain in 1973, thousands of dead fish appeared in the harbour. The cause was the detergent used to clean up the exhibition site.

A large blue whale needs 3 tons of food every day.

A group of jellyfish is called a smack.

Birds don't urinate.

Homing pigeons can exceed 90mph (144.84 km/h).

GRAB YOUR FREE BONUS BOOK HERE

Get ready to laugh-out-loud with your **FREE GIFT - '201 One-Liners and Short Jokes'** – your ultimate source of chuckles and titters!

Click HERE or scan the QR code to receive your gag-tastic e-book, on the house! And that's not all – you'll join

The 1001 One-Liner Club for FREE and receive a weekly light-hearted email to kickstart your Monday mornings with a smile!

WOULD YOU LIKE TO DO ME

A BIG FAVOUR?

I hope very much that you enjoyed this book and learned something new.

I would be very grateful if you could leave a review for **The Ultimate Trivia Collection**. Reviews not only help other readers discover the kinds of books they want to read, but also help support the author.

All you have to do is to go online to the retailer where you bought this book. Then go to the customer review section and leave your comments.

Thank you so much.

DO YOU LIKE READING BOOKS?

WOULD YOU LIKE US TO SEND YOU FREE BOOKS?

The publishers of this book would love you to join their Advance Readers Club. All members receive free e-books on all sorts of interesting subjects which have included puppy care, cookbooks and joke books, prior to the book being marketed globally.

All we ask you to do is to read through it and then leave an honest review on Amazon.

Please email us at *info@chascannco.com* or scan the QR code to be added to our VIP list of readers. *Your email address is protected – it will never be divulged to third parties.*

The 1001 One-Liners and Dad Jokes range.
Laughter is the best therapy!
A truly hilarious romp through the best one-liners ever!

Please scan the QR code below to grab your copy.

For more popular books on *HUMOUR, LIFESTYLE, BUSINESS* and a varied range of *COLOURING BOOKS FOR GROWN-UPS*

please visit

www.chascannco.com